Leadership Lessons from Life

Heartwarming Stories of How Small Gestures Make a Big Difference

H. Jim Miller

I have dedicated this book to my family: my wife Susan, our daughter Karri, and sons Bill and Casey, their spouses Jason, Mindy and Jenna. And to our two granddaughters Payton and Gracie, who have made our lives complete.

Table of Contents

Introduction

Thank you for purchasing and reading this book. It is my sincere hope that the stories that follow will warm your heart and ignite a spark for you to yearn for and treat others in the similar manner as described in each story.

If you are a leader, manager, or an administrator in an organization, business, or an educational institution, I urge you to set aside the organizational agenda for a minute and focus on people. General George S. Patton said, "Never tell people how to do things, tell them what to do and they will surprise you with their ingenuity." Effective leaders build a culture where associates can thrive individually so that the sum total of individual efforts can make an organization successful.

The following stories are true, and some names have been changed to protect those still living and influencing others. I trust that this book can be helpful as you interact with those around you.

Leadership Lessons from Life

By

H. Jim Miller

Chapter 1 – Who Am I?

"One's past is what one is"................. *Oscar Wilde*

Reflecting over the past 50 years proved to be an enlightened exercise of lessons life has afforded me and introduced me to who I am. More notably, I was able to examine leadership examples, good and bad, that have shaped my approach to life. Leadership is something that by definition will stand out clearly if one simply is observant. This reflection has instilled a curiosity in me that has encouraged me to analyze these examples in detail to determine what they have really meant. At times the negative principle of a particular leadership trait was used; sometimes so poorly that I could learn the correct principal by default.

We were a family of limited means, Mom had a high school education and Dad had an hourly non-professional job. Being an ambitious kid, I approached Dad one day and asked him if I could get an afternoon paper route. I was ten years old, and he encouraged me to give it a try. So I went to the phone book, looked up the number of the local newspaper and gave them a call. The lady on the other end of the line asked me right off the bat how old I was,

when I responded that I was ten, she told me "Nice try, you will have

to wait until you are eleven years old." Being rather persistent, I

asked her if I could get a route when I turned eleven and she said,

"Sure, call back next year." The card up my sleeve was that I was

turning eleven in just two short months. A couple of months later I

turned eleven years old, called up the newspaper again and requested

the newspaper route that I had thought they had promised to me. I

did not know if I was talking to the same lady, but she told me this

time that she was placing my name on a list and for me to wait for a

call. Unbeknownst to an eleven year old, I had to wait for an

opening to develop and then the opening had to be juxtaposed to my

home. I became frustrated, of course, and was ready to give up on

the idea. My dad encouraged me to contact the lady by phone again

in a week, introduce myself politely, and ask her to please remember

me when an opening developed in my area. I did this for three or

four weeks, and then lo and behold, I received a call that a small

route was open right next to my home and it was mine if I wanted it.

Of course I accepted, eventually keeping that paper route for six years and even adding a second one within that time, allowing me to make some excellent money for a teenager.

One might wonder why I had a route for six years, especially when the turnover was usually high among unreliable teens. That was because my parents would not allow me to give it up until I was hired for a so called "real job." Since the minimum age for a real job was usually 16, I knew that I would have this thing for at least five years, so I made the best of it. My parents encouraged, and usually forced me to supply superior customer service, deliver the paper early, and collect the monthly bill from each customer in a timely fashion so that the monthly invoice due to the company on the tenth of each month could be paid on time. They stressed that keeping customers happy was critical to making money. They explained that this was a learning experience, and these were principles I needed to master in order to be successful. Sure enough, these principles served me well when it came time to search for that real job, one I would eventually keep for eight years. These principles of dealing face-to-face with customers, providing that service which would bring the patron back for more; reliability, punctuality, stewardship of money and resources, afforded me the skills to earn my way though college debt-free, buy a home at age 21, and travel internationally. These lessons have shaped my working career and have led to some success. Concurrently, and early on, my parents would purchase books for me on success, attitude, and biographies of successful businessmen. Those seeds which they planted for future success piqued my interest and led to greater achievements than I would have achieved on my own.

Dad continuously modeled behavior that he wanted me to learn and adopt as I grew older. A motto of his was; "Treat others with respect and dignity and they will return it to you." As a young child (and also true today), I was a rabid Los Angeles Dodger fan. One summer evening, my father and I were walking up Figueroa St. in Los Angeles in 1959-1960, on our way to a Dodger game. This was during the era of civil rights dissension, and unrest in many inner cities was common. In those days the Los Angeles Memorial Coliseum was also used for Dodger baseball, and Coliseum parking was nearly non-existent. Dad preferred to park a mile or two away and walk. It was free, it provided exercise and little did I know until years later, it afforded Dad the opportunity to model behaviors he wanted me to embrace as I was growing up. In those days, the Dodgers gave away weekly souvenirs provided by the Union Oil Company, such as a water color portrait or booklet on each player. Being a fan of our great national pastime, I of course acquired these passionately for my growing collection of memorabilia at home. There was a Union 76 gas station on the way to the Los Angeles Coliseum where the Dodgers played in South Los Angeles. There was a black gentleman who worked there, and Dad had already developed a relationship with him from previous visits to get these weekly souvenirs for me. If the team was out of town and we missed the giveaway, this gentleman would save the souvenirs for me for when my Dad or both of us would attend a following ballgame. On one particular night, we arrived at the gas station on the way to the ball park. Dad greeted the attendant and introduced me. We chatted for several minutes, and I answered questions about school, hobbies, and what I wanted to be when I grew up. Since Dad had been longstanding acquaintance of this man, this man was interested in me. He wished me luck in the future and reminded me to do well in and stay in school. He handed us the portraits, we thanked him, and he promised to save more pictures for us if we didn't make it back to a game for a while. On the way up the street, Dad turned to me and pointed out that by treating people with dignity and respect they would return it. He emphasized that people of all colors were the same, and treating them with dignity and respect was the right thing to do[1]. He treated all people this way, and continuously set that example for his children and grandchildren.

Great Leaders:
1. Set a proper example for others to follow.
2. Treat others with dignity and respect.
3. Individualize each person.
4. Plant seeds for success
5. Teach reliability, punctuality, stewardship of money, and customer service.
6. Build on past experiences

Chapter 2 – An Introduction to the Real World

"Don't find fault, find a remedy"...............*Henry Ford*

My first job proved to be a jarring introduction to the real

world. Sometimes, and maybe more often than we realize, a situation

may arise where we can turn a poor leadership example into a

learning experience. The paper route that I was hired for at age

eleven proved to be a learning experience almost immediately. I had

been on the job for about two weeks, just enough time to get

comfortable with the routine, when I first encountered my

supervisor. My supervisor was a man named John, a Persian who

had immigrated to the United States a few years earlier. I soon

discovered that he employed oppressive managerial techniques with

his paper carriers, all of whom averaged about 12 or 13 years of age.

John was like a dog barking at you for hours; he was belligerent and

condescending.[2] John dropped off the stack of daily newspapers one

day and told me that he wanted a route list, "tomorrow or else." I

had no clue what a route list was, he did not explain it to me, so as

an eleven year old kid would most likely do, I forgot about it. Bear

in mind that this was 1964, there was no computerization, and this newspaper evidently had no record of who its customers were. During his newspaper delivery on the following day, John requested, not so nicely, the route list. When I told him that I did not have it, he grew angry, pointed his finger squarely in my face and proceeded to tell me that I would be fired if I did not have the list the following day. I discussed this situation with my mom after I delivered that day's papers, and she said that we had "…probably better put a list together." As we drove the route, I pointed out each house along the way that subscribed to the paper, and we made a list that we gave him the next day. John got his way, but at an expense -- he established acrimony between himself and his carriers, which undoubtedly led to decreased production. I learned from this experience that this style of management is usually counter-productive, depresses morale, and creates increased turnover. It is the manager's job to make people feel as if they are glad to come to work every day, and John didn't seem to understand this concept. He eventually left the position, and I continued being a paper boy for more than five additional years, under much better leadership.

Great Leaders:
1. Encourage and praise workers.
2. Exhibit patience.
3. Build productive relationships.

Chapter 3 – Gotta Be In Shape

"High expectations are the key to everything"...............Sam Walton

After attending junior high school in a rough area of town, and vividly remembering what my dad told me upon entering seventh grade, I did not know what to expect next. Dad said upon my apprehension of being bussed to the junior high across town, "Don't worry, kids carried knives when I was in junior high too." I did not find that very comforting. However that feeling was soon tempered a little by my physical education teacher, Coach Eichorn. Coach was an advocate of physical conditioning, and wasted no time introducing us to physical pain during calisthenics. Before we could start the seasonal sport games we looked forward to, we had a set of exercises he led us through, followed by a run around the softball backstop about an eighth of a mile away. One day I took it easy, and came jogging back rather nonchalantly. Coach approached me and pointed out that another kid who was quite obese handily beat me back to our assigned numbers on the blacktop. I was honest, and told him that I was not really trying very hard. Coach Eichorn, although probably only in his mid twenties, calmly told me that was the obstacle that kept most people from being successful. "If you just try as hard as you can at everything" he said, "You will be more successful; you could have easily beaten that other kid with a little effort." Because he made a personal connection with me, his admonition meant something to me, he had credibility. By caring for me in a significant way, Coach Eichorn helped me grow and actualize myself [3]. Fast forward 41 years, I am at the computer at the kitchen table while my wife is flipping through the channels on the television. I hear a voice on a news channel from a man being interviewed by a news reporter. I jumped up from the table and head for the living room, I asked her to go back to the previous channel, and sure enough there was Coach Eichorn being interviewed on the news about an event that he witnessed in Los Angeles. How did I remember his voice? It was the 360 P. E. classes I had with him over two years in junior high where we had engrained into our minds "One two three ONE, one two three TWO, one two three THREE!......KEEP THOSE ARMS UP! One two three FOUR.........NO CHEATING ON THOSE JUMPING JACKS!"

A vivid colorful memory instantly appeared in my mind of those years in junior high school, and only after 40-plus years was I mature enough to appreciate the experience of being influenced by Coach Eichorn. I have thought of him scores of times over the years, especially after I have found one of my own students not trying very hard. I find myself repeating his admonition from decades past, "If you just try as hard as you can at everything you will be more successful." I hope I have been as influential with my students as he was with me.

Without warning, I experience what seems to be a paranormal type of phenomena I cannot quite explain. It occurs three to four times a year, without explanation. It seems that I have some sort of extra sensory contact with someone that occurs when I think of or see someone who looks like them, or as in this case, I saw Coach Eichorn on television. It only occurs however, if it has been a long period since I have actually seen them. Additionally I have learned to forget about the fact that I was just reminded of them, because if I go looking for them they will not appear. I did just that. Three or four months later, I arrived at my high school reunion to celebrate with classmates our 35th year since graduating from high school. I made the rounds greeting old friends, proudly showing the latest pictures of the granddaughters, exchanging yarns of our experiences since our last encounter, when baseball teammate Ruben interrupted me and asked "Jimmy did you see Coach Eichorn?" "He's here?!" I replied. Ruben then led me over to where he was surrounded by half a dozen people who, just like me, were greatly influenced by this man. I marveled at what I saw. This man who must now be in his late 60's was not much different than the last time I saw him some 30 plus years earlier. He was the picture of health, fit and trim, posture ramrod straight, as if he had been a career marine (although I don't think he was ever in the service). Man, it was great to see him. I waited in line behind Bob, a classmate since elementary school. When Bob was thanking Coach for being such a great influence on his life, I realized that I was not alone, but only one of probably hundreds who felt the same way. As is customary at a function like this, we were all wearing name tags with our high school picture on it for obvious reasons. Coach stared at my picture, saw the name and warmly, with a smile of "glad to see you Jimmy," and gave me an embrace. We discussed the incident where the obese kid outran me because I was not trying, and Coach immediately said, "You know, I remember that." I thanked him for

the lesson and reminded him that his influence has touched many,

especially me and those onto whom I may pass his wisdom. I now

certainly hope he will be at our next reunion as well.

Great Leaders:
1. Instruct
2. Connect
3. Correct

Chapter 4 – Culture Sets the Tone

"Leadership is a potent combination of strategy and character"...............*Norman Schwarzkopf*

After surviving two years at junior high with the daily apprehension that everyone is probably armed but me, I was really apprehensive about the next step. On my first day of high school in September 1967 I entered a brand new building without knowing what to expect. It was a daunting day for a shy kid of 14 who could barely look an adult in the eye when they were talking to me. Although I would not realize it until several years later, the moment I walked into fifth period World History my life would change forever. My teacher, Mr. Beck, was a brand new teacher of 23 and straight out of student teaching. What I would learn as the year dragged on was that this person was a man of character and integrity, and that he was what I envisioned my father to have been at the same age. This was probably a major reason why I hit it off so well with Mr. Beck. He treated everyone with respect and dignity, and most importantly, treated all students fairly. "Rules are rules", as the saying goes, and I found this out the hard way. I was removed from

17

class one day for "excessive classroom disturbance". In those days that simply meant talking in class. After being sequestered in the counselor's office for several days, I returned to his class with a stern admonition that it will not happen again. It didn't. The thing that stayed with me was that he treated me as a person of value; with respect and the expectation that I was going to live up to my potential and he was going to make sure that I produced what I was capable of. I did my best in my ninth grade year because of Mr. Beck, and played for him on the freshman baseball team. I learned a great deal about world history and baseball because Coach Beck established a relationship with me. Little did I know this would lead to a 40 plus year odyssey that still continues today.

At the end of my freshman year, he was drafted into the U.S. Army for a two year stint. In 1968 this meant that he was headed for war. Being a 14 year old kid, I really didn't even understand what Vietnam was, why we were there, or even where it was on the map, but Mr. Beck told us that he would see us again in two years and expected us to continue what he taught us during the past year. Years later, I would realize that he meant something more than the world history he taught us. He wanted us to continue to lead lives of character and integrity while he was gone. As we eagerly awaited his return, the school kept the student body apprised of correspondence he sent, so we at least knew that he was safe. However, since all we had was postal mail delivery in the 1960's, we mainly wondered where he was and how he was doing. Those two years came and went, and Mr. Beck was back for the start of our senior year. He was the same in demeanor as when he left, and told us that he was proud to serve our country, and that he hoped if anyone of us were called that we would honorably do the same. He constantly set an example of high character and integrity, and quietly expected others to do the same. During my senior year, he was the Key Club advisor where I served as president. Key Club is a high school version of Kiwanis International, a service club. One of the requirements he placed on the club was that we were to become involved with the physically handicapped students at a nearby elementary school. Every week during lunch, our club members would walk to the school and bring the students, in their wheelchairs, back to the high school library. We would help them check out books and return them to their school within the hour. We learned that even though some people had physical challenges, they had minds that needed feeding just as we did. This leadership lesson has stayed with me all these years. He introduced us to a situation that he knew would be character building for us, and beneficial for those less fortunate. He constantly gave of himself, and this gesture taught us to be the ones who give first, especially to those who needed it. Wheeling the kids in their wheelchairs opened us up to another world that we did not even know existed. Most of these students were imprisoned by their physical limitations and we were able to extend freedom to them every week or two for an hour. Today, I still feel the warmth of each student's "Thank you for taking me to the library today, hope to see you again." This was the last time I took my good health and free mobility for granted, and realized this impact on me every time I had a physically challenged student in my own classroom. Mr. Beck continued that practice until he retired from teaching. In the four decades I have known him, Mr. Beck has lived an uncommonly open life, never judgmental of others.

A couple of years ago Mr. Beck retired from teaching and coaching baseball after forty years in the same classroom, at the same school and coaching on the same field. His wife called to invite me to attend a retirement party for 'Bob', as she referred to him, but I was under orders to keep it a secret. That was because he would not want any attention. Mrs. Beck set the party up by tricking him into going to another function nearby. When they arrived for the surprise, there were over 150 people there to greet Mr. Beck – mostly former students like myself. We each gladly paid the $20 admission fee for a simple meal and for a scholarship fund that would be established in his name to help an economically disadvantaged teen go to college. We all knew that he would not accept any gifts and would rather help someone else instead. This event was reminiscent of the 1996 movie *Mr. Holland's Opus*, where the popular high school band teacher was forced to retire, and scores of former students returned to his school to play a symphony with him one last time. This was a love fest to honor a man who meant something to hundreds of people. Mrs. Beck designed the party agenda to be a chronology of his life, from childhood to retirement. Once his life was celebrated and she read about a dozen letters of well-wishers who could not attend the gathering, she opened up the microphone to those of us who wanted to speak about what he has meant to us in our lives. Fortunately we were able to honor a man who has meant so much, and set such a good example for us while he was still with us, that was the beauty of having this party. I was able to tell him that he was one of the two or three primary role models in my life behind my late father. I am sure that there were others with the same sentiments.

Today Mr. Beck is enjoying retirement with his wife, raising two young school age children, with plenty of time to be a sterling example for them as he was for us 40 years before. When I see him today, I still get that hearty smile, the firm handshake, and questions about how everything is going. His lesson in leadership is his concern and desire to help others less fortunate than he, and his demeanor constant. He even writes with the same Parker pens that he used in the 1960's proving he has been a dependable constant for decades for those of us who have known him.

Chapter 5 – Heartbreak

"A man must be big enough to admit his mistakes, smart enough to profit from them, and strong enough to correct them"……………….John C. Maxwell

My high school years proved to be challenging, but even more rewarding as I discovered that role models were all around me. As a teenager matures, he or she will encounter a plethora of emotions as both the psyche and body mature. Proper role models are essential for a young person as they graduate from adolescence to adulthood. One of these role models for me was Mr. Lyle Fry, the principal of my high school. Mr. Fry made it a point of personally knowing every student and in some cases their families. In our school of 1,100 students that was possible. I had known Mr. Fry personally for four years when our basketball team, of which I was a member, found ourselves in the playoffs for the state championship. The school wanted to stage a rally to pump up the team and the students for that playoff game. However in the spirit of academic achievement, Mr. Fry vetoed the effort. He called me into his office to explain his rationale, and asked me to pass it to the team, and that we would have one for the next game because he was confident we would win that evening. As luck would have it, we lost the game that night 71-69 in triple overtime. The team, the school, and especially Mr. Fry were devastated over the loss, but Mr. Fry took it personally. He had me call a meeting of the fallen players so that he could address the team face to face. In true leadership fashion, Mr. Fry apologized to our coach and each player personally. He took the blame for our loss that night, now somehow feeling that a rally would have helped us win. We lost the game but I gained a life long friend. This friendship lasted for over 40 years until Mr. Fry's passing a couple of years ago. This leadership style employed by Mr. Fry gained everyone's respect and devotion during his life. Because of the lessons I learned from Mr. Fry after that basketball game, I yearned to contact his sons and express my condolences. Mr. Fry modeled the behavior many of us followed in subsequent years and that was to confront an issue head on. I felt compelled to share with his sons, those lessons I learned and to express gratitude that Mr. Fry made an impact on many lives especially my own. Once I tracked them down across the country, they were not surprised to hear my tale; because their dad would have done the same thing I did by searching and finding them to express my gratitude.

Great Leaders:
1. Take defeat personally.
2. Take the blame when things go awry.
3. Pass out praise with success.
4. Express gratitude.

Chapter 6 – Taken Under His Wing

"Few things are harder to put up with than the annoyance of a good example" ....Mark Twain

Concurrent with the leadership modeling of Mr. Fry, my high school career was replete with other role models as well. One in particular, Mr. Joe Medure, was my biology teacher and a class advisor. Being a new and relatively small school, the advisors worked to establish an effective student government, and to exploit the talents of student leaders. Evidently, Mr. Medure thought I qualified as one of those leaders. Being a shy 16 year old, timid and self -conscious, I heartily disagreed. I wanted no part of student government, public speaking; especially, voicing my opinion. Mr. Medure would not listen to any of my objections, but insisted that I run for office and he would assist me. Because of my respect and trust in Mr. Medure, I finally agreed. He entered me in the race for athletic commissioner, and worked with me on a campaign speech. I really think that he just didn't care for the incumbent and wanted me to run against him. But we honed the speech over several lunch periods; I practiced it in front of the mirror, until he felt that I was ready to go. What he didn't tell me was that I would be giving the speech to the 1,100 mostly rowdy and irreverent people that made up the student body. Mr. Medure was positive, encouraging, and empathetic, but most of all caring and right by my side. He evidently saw in me some characteristics that indicated leadership potential, and he wanted to bring that out, even if I didn't know I had it myself. He led me over the imaginary barriers that we all place before ourselves when we are unsure of the future outcome. But Mr. Medure had traveled this road before, and knew what the outcome would be, even though I was too inexperienced to visualize it myself. I eventually lost the election by six votes, and felt pretty discouraged. Mr. Medure however was ecstatic and I grew even more confused. He accentuated that I indeed had won; I won because of the experience. I wrote and delivered a speech to an audience of over a thousand people; I broke through the fear of public speaking and nearly won the election. He stressed that it is the experience one should be after and the desired outcomes would take care of themselves. Mr. Medure established a trusting relationship with me and many other students over the years. During my tenth grade academic year, my grandfather died and I needed to miss school to attend his memorial service, however I had my mom take me to school so as not to miss Mr. Medure's biology class the day of the funeral. He left that type of life-long impression with me.

As luck would have it, or maybe it was fate, I was hired by Mr. Medure to teach biology at my old high school some 26 years later. During one of my annual evaluations he merely suggested that I provide a sample of a poster I was having the biology students make of a human body system. Due to the tremendous trust and respect he earned from me, I considered his request gospel. I went home that night and made a poster of that body system from cut outs, word processing labels and colored clip art on the subject. I had the school laminate the poster and it was available for the students to use it as a guide the next day. Soon I had made posters for all of the body systems we would be covering that year putting in scores of hours to complete them, life-like and in vivid color. On a subsequent evaluation he raved over the series of subject appropriate posters that would help the students learn each system. Mr. Medure complimented me on the posters, my time commitment to complete them, and even gave me the credit for the idea. He was secure enough with himself to give me the credit for his suggestion in order to get his goals accomplished. That goal was to help make me a more effective teacher. He accomplished this and earned more respect as a person in the process. This enabling structure employed by Mr. Medure helped me succeed. He didn't monitor my behavior to insure compliance. [4] I intuitively feel that had he monitored my behavior to insure compliance with what he wanted, the end result would not have been as comprehensive. [5]

This trusting relationship he established with me earned him my greatest respect. He could be trusted, and that earned him respect from hundreds of students and colleagues. Because he freely gave us respect, time, and resources to do the job, he earned our trust. [6]

Great Leaders:
1. Work on goals.
2. Hand out compliments.
3. Let others have the credit.
4. Allow creative freedom.
5. Establish trusting relationships.
6. Leave life-long impressions.
7. Teach that the experience is what is important.

Chapter 7 - Oops

"The question isn't who is going to let me, it's who is going to stop me"...........Ayn Rand

Because Dad was reared in the 1920's, and learned to work hard because of the Great Depression, he believed that one should always have a job no matter what. Consequently, my parents would not allow me to leave the aforementioned paper route until I had procured a so called "real job." He suggested that I work in a grocery store as a way to pay for college because the earnings were better than minimum wage, it came with good benefits, and there was always a need for grocery stores. He explained that I should apply at seven to ten stores, find out who exactly was charged with the hiring at each store, and then visit that person and no one else once per week until I had a job. Working in the grocery business himself, he knew that managers dealt the applications off of the top of the stack, so there was a greater probability of being hired if I had the most recent contact with the actual individual in charge of hiring new employees. Further, he lamented that these managers always worked on Saturdays because it was usually the busiest day of the week. Off I went and eventually applied at eight local grocery stores. Two of the managers told me to not to waste my time, that they had no interest in hiring anyone in the near future so I was left with six prospective places of employment. My father taught me how to approach a manager by calling him by name, always mister or miss, offering a firm handshake, and to simply say "I am interested in working for you, and I would appreciate it if you would consider me when an opening develops." I found this surprisingly easy, and it worked in only about two and a half weeks. This was because in business there is a significantly higher chance that a manager is going to hire someone that they are already familiar with. In my case I simply made myself familiar with six grocery store managers and Gene was the first one who had an opening. I walked into the market one Thursday afternoon after school when Gene summoned me over as he saw me enter the store. He said "Jim", as he waved me over, "drop in on Saturday morning at nine and I might have something for you." We shook hands and I left eager to return in a couple of days wondering what he really had in mind for me.

On Saturday I returned promptly at nine adorned in a dress shirt and tie just in case he wanted me to start that day. Instead he welcomed me to the market, and handed me a schedule of hours for the following week. I was scheduled to work on Tuesday, Thursday, Saturday, and Sunday. I arrived early on Tuesday; Gene gave me an orientation of the store, introduced me to my coworkers, and gave me a brief description of my position as a box boy. I worked industriously on that first day hoping that I did well enough to continue since there was a six month probationary period. When I returned to work on Thursday, Gene called me aside and explained, rather professionally, that a large order that I had bagged on Tuesday ended up on a customer's driveway after she returned home from the store. Gene, in order to pacify and retain her as a customer, went to her home, cleaned up the mess and replaced the broken bottles of groceries that resulted from the overloaded bags that I had filled. Fortunately Gene was more than a manager, he was a leader. I was ready for the axe, but Gene took me aside and explained that I should have received more initial training, and that it was not my fault. He modeled for me the basics of the job, told me that he was right there if I needed additional help and that I should not hesitate to ask for his assistance. This gesture was the first step in building trust with a new employee. He expounded that he was impressed with the methods I used to get the job at his store and he could see my potential as a valued employee. Needless to say I was happy to hear that, but thankful as well that he was a leader with substance. Gene rewarded me for what he could see under the surface, knowing that I was taught well from someone with experience: my dad. I worked for Gene for five years until he was transferred to another store.

There was more evidence though of Gene's leadership of rewarding employees for hard and diligent work. Jesse was the store's custodian, and exhibited a tireless work ethic. Jesse, his wife Jessie and their three children emigrated from Mexico a few years before. Jesse only spoke limited English, but it was evident that he was hired as custodian due to his immutable work ethic. I observed him working like no one I had ever witnessed. As I got to know Jesse over the first few months that I was there, I came to admire him and his wife greatly. Jesse and his wife were a couple with stellar character and integrity, and were intent on providing a good life for their kids. He told me that his greatest honor was to be able to come to America where opportunity was unlimited. He believed that hard work was the key to success. Sure enough, Gene our manager recognized what Jesse believed. After several years as custodian, Gene asked Jesse if he would like to become a meat cutter. I remember standing in the office doorway when Gene told me of the new plans in store for Jesse and feeling terrific that this man of character was being given such a great opportunity. One of the most motivating incentives is simply a leader who personally congratulates an employee for doing a good job. [7] Talk about personal congratulations, this element of praise changed Jesse and his family's life forever. Giving effective awards is a key in continued stellar work performance from an employee. [8] This certainly was a just reward for Jesse's years in the custodial ranks. In the days of the 70's, meat cutters made higher wages than a regular grocery clerk. Gene, being a former meat cutter himself knew what kind of lifestyle a meat cutter's wage could provide, and since there were five people in Jesse's family, it could be an excellent opportunity for him. Jesse accepted and went to apprentice training and eventually enjoyed a long career as a meat cutter prior to retirement. The leadership of Gene, in rewarding Jesse for his hard and productive work, enabled this family to enjoy a higher standard of living than they ever imagined. I learned from Jesse, that perseverance and hard work does pay off, and I have tried to follow his example for the 40 years I have known him.

This diligent work ethic is simply a manifestation of this man's character. He gives the credit to Gene for giving him the opportunity, and has mentioned to me several times that he owes his success to Gene. I have known Jesse for the past 40 years and these qualities have been evident in his children and grandchildren. In fact, I had his grandson as a student a few years ago, and could see Jesse in him. This was a man who led by example for his family and friends to see, and it has served him well.

Great Leaders:
1. Reward achievement
2. Train instead of admonish
3. Build trust

Chapter 8 – Working Side by Side

"Example is leadership".........................*Albert Schweitzer*

Upon leaving college in 1977, I went into sales with a
Fortune 100 Company headquartered in Camden, New Jersey. Ken
was the local manager assigned to me in Southern California. The
first thing Ken did was to establish a trusting working relationship
with colleagues and his representatives; I was no different. On my
first day on the job, Ken greeted me in the office with a smile and a
firm handshake, and then said "Let's go have breakfast." Off to
Denny's we went, and Ken proceeded to give me an orientation of
what to expect. He was quick to let me know that he was looking
forward to working with me, and that I would be learning how to sell
product right along side of him. He would work with me daily for
the first four weeks and I would get hands-on experience. That I did.
Ken worked with me step-by-step, and then allowed me to work a
little on my own with him nearby. At the end of the day, we would
go get a soft drink and he would review my progress. This proved to

be an effective tool with me, because I respond well to modeled

behavior. It was so effective that I was awarded the largest account

in the West within a year. Ken taught me well. He made it a point

to make sure that I knew that everyone at a customer's office was

important, from the forklift driver to the president. He modeled this

behavior for me when I received the responsibility for the large

grocery company account. This proved to be invaluable as I called

on that account for three years. John C. Maxwell calls this the "law

of connection." [9] Ken explained that everyone is important,

especially in business. "You never know who can be of help to

you," he said, "and knowing everyone is vital."

U. S. Army General Norman Schwarzkopf was known to be

a soldier's general. With the country at war during the holidays in

1991, Schwarzkopf explained how he tried to make the troops feel

like they were at home while they were in the mess hall:

> "I shook hands with everyone in the line, went
> behind the serving counter to greet the cooks and
> helpers, and worked my way through the mess hall,
> hitting every table, wishing everyone Merry
> Christmas. Then I went into the second and third
> dining facilities and did the same thing. I came back
> to the first mess tent and repeated the exercise,
> because by that time there was an entirely new set of
> faces. Then I sat down with some of the troops and

had my dinner. In the course of four hours, I must have shaken a thousand hands." [10]

A man of this stature, General Schwarzkopf didn't have to do this, but this was his method of effectively connecting with his subordinates. Ken showed me how to make these connections in the business setting. Tom Peters, author of the 1980's epic business work, *In Search of Excellence*, calls this MBWA, managing by walking around. [11]

What was more important, though, was that Ken established a relationship with me and exploited that relationship to foster my talents to help me develop the proper business sense. Although the office was about 30 miles from my home, Ken and I lived only about a mile or two apart. On my first day, Ken gave me a ride home because my company car had yet to arrive at the office. Instead of taking me straight home Ken drove to his house so that I could meet his wife Barbie (yes, they were really Ken and Barbie). He introduced me as one of his new guys, and that he was excited to have me working with him. From there, he drove me home so he could meet my wife and family. Always personable and hospitable, my wife, Susan, invited him in for coffee and we discussed my new job. Ken established this new relationship quickly, and solidified

our professional relationship, along with a personal relationship with

our spouses. This relationship was strong, deep, and solid until

Ken's untimely and sudden death from heart disease some ten years

later

Ken was a horseman, helping his daughter raise and show

horses. I will forever remember an image of Ken in my mind

standing on the side of the road heading up to the local mountains.

Ken was standing there with shovel in hand, wearing a straw hat,

blue jeans, field boots, and holding a garden hose and a bucket. He

was waiting for me and a buddy to pick him up to go to the

mountains where a fire was threatening our tiny out-of-the-way

cabin. Ken and I had been working together that day, when we

heard a radio report about three in the afternoon of a fire sweeping

through the area where our cabin was located. There were Santa

Ana Westerly winds in the area that day, and as the weather was

clear, we could see the mountain range from where we were working

some 20 miles to the south. Ken was with me in my car, and said

"let's go and take care of the cabin." We drove back, set a meeting

place, and went home for our work clothes. Later, we picked up Ken and headed to the cabin. About a mile from our property the local authorities prevented us from proceeding further due to the fire danger. The good news is the cabin escaped damage, as the wind changed direction and pushed the fire away from the village where our property was located. Through this event, we learned of the compassionate side of Ken. He was willing to help two guys he worked with to save their property if need be. He established that our needs were a priority to him, and he was ready and able to assist. His leadership example made us want to work for him, and made us willing to return the favor whenever he needed it. He initiated the relational bridge between us and led with his heart, and that demonstrated how much he cared about his people. Not coincidently, he made sure that we did not get in trouble for leaving work two hours early.

Great Leaders:
  1. Care about their people.
  2. Have concern for the individual.
  3. Initiate relationships

Chapter 9 – Integrity is the Key

"In striving for your objective you'll discover hidden strengths you didn't know you had"..*John Fuhrman*

Prior to entering the field of education, I earned my living from commission sales in the surgical device industry. George Sjodin was a dapper gent of Swedish descent, reared on a Minnesota farm and brought his strong work ethic to the business field. As a regional manager, he was responsible for sales and service with ten representative subordinates. As a former accountant, George was highly organized and very quantitative. More importantly, George was honest, engaging and concerned about each of our individual successes. This was evident on the first day that I met him. I had a job interview with George scheduled for two in the afternoon, and arrived several minutes early to make a good impression. I strolled into the Howard Johnson's hotel at 1:40 PM for the interview, and George promptly met me in the lobby with a hearty handshake and a warm, generous smile. I learned from this initial meeting that George was obsessively early for everything. This was an interview like no other I had ever experienced. In the business world, it is common for an interview to be highly structured, politically correct and almost clinical. When one leaves the meeting, they are usually told to wait for a phone call to see if a second interview will be scheduled. But with George, this interview was about me, about how my goals in life could be achieved by working for him and this company. He gave me a brief history about the company, showed me aerial pictures of the factories and main offices in New Jersey, and talked only briefly about the product line. I learned that George was about people, about how he would work with us to achieve our objectives, and how that in turn would help make the company successful. The two and a half hours that I spent with George, seemed like only a few minutes, and I left knowing that I had the job. The second interview a couple of weeks later included George's boss, Dave, who was the company's Western Area Vice President. Dave conducted the interview much like the conventional interviews I had been on with other companies. Dave ended the interview by simply saying "We'll let you know." However, at the conclusion, George walked me out to my car and told me that I did good job, and that he would call me that evening. As promised, George called that evening and invited my wife and me to dinner that weekend at his country club with him and his wife. Of course we accepted, and met him at the club for dinner. Upon arrival George was waiting for us at the entry way of the country club. He had arranged valet parking in advance, and upon our arrival, escorted us into the dining room where we met his wife Carolyn. The four of us had a cordial dinner, engaging conversation, and began to develop a genuinely warm relationship. George, we could tell, did have an agenda for the evening, as he asked questions of my wife about her support of my career, prodded her to carefully consider what kind of impact this profession would have on our family life. He was looking for her support for what I was going to be doing because he knew, from his decades of experience, the value of a supportive spouse. After a couple of hours, George and Carolyn walked us back to the valet parking kiosk where we retrieved our car and made the two hour sojourn back home. As we navigated the rain slicked streets towards home, my wife and I discussed and pondered what it would be like to work for a man like this, a man such as I never had before as a boss. We realized that trust and integrity foster prosperity, [12] which lead us to feel comfortable with George and the company. As we pulled into the driveway, we agreed that we would love to get a job offer to work for George.

Early the following week, we received a hand written letter from George expressing how nice our evening had been for him and Carolyn, and that they were looked forward to a long, rewarding, and mutually beneficial relationship. He knew the value of giving praise and recognition in writing.[13] On the next day, I received a phone call with a job offer from George that began an eight year personal and professional relationship.

At this company, professional trainers provided initial orientation in the field for several weeks prior to the representatives attending formal training at company headquarters in Wayne, New Jersey. As our regional sales manager, George was responsible for our success once we were back in our own territory; however he went above and beyond the call of duty and kept in twice weekly contact with me to make sure that I was comfortable with the process and to answer any questions I might have about my new career. What George was doing was building a strong foundational footing for our personal relationship, knowing that -- from years of experience -- it would lead to professional success. He knew that developing good people depended on his willingness to support and encourage them. [14] Again George was working his agenda, one that would have me hitting the ground running when I returned from training. He used to say that he was always trying to put ten pounds of flour in a five pound sack, which was true about the training that I endured, so his emphasis on our relationship while I was away was a morale booster, and he knew that.

Back in the field after training was a challenge, but George worked side by side with me for several weeks. Soon like a mother eagle with her chick, he kicked me out of the nest for a couple of days, and then met up with me again. Like the chick learning how to fly, he rescued me before I hit the ground. The next time he booted me out of the nest, I flew a little better, and before I knew it I was on my own. As a trained representative, I was alone until George came out to work with us for two consecutive days about every five weeks. That was time with George all of his representatives looked forward to.

When George worked with us, he acted like our partner rather than our boss. He knew what our yearly and quarterly objectives were, so he set out to help us achieve them instead of checking on us to see if we were doing everything just right. If there was an area of improvement he felt needed to be addressed, he simply said, "Try this it has worked for me in the past, it might work for you also." Because we trusted George, we knew what he told us would work for us, too. During our yearly evaluation period each spring, George handed out the evaluation forms and instructed us to give careful thought to our previous year's performance and to objectively evaluate ourselves in each category, and then plan comprehensively for the upcoming year. When the evaluation meeting arrived his work was done for him. He invariably found that each employee more critically evaluated themselves than he had. Their goals for the upcoming year were higher than what George envisioned, and all formulated more detailed plans than were expected. What George demonstrated was that by allowing sufficient time for the employee to plan his work, he could then work his plan more productively, and with ownership. [15] This enabling structure was a win-win situation for the company and the employee. Employee productivity was high and morale was good, and this produced positive outcomes. [15]

Part way through my eight year tenure with the company, I left for another opportunity. When that didn't work out as I had planned, I called George to ask him if I could use him as a reference for another potential opportunity in the same field. To my surprise he said, "How would you like to come back to work for me?" I was thrilled and went through the interview process again, and was eventually placed in an adjacent territory to the one that I left the year before. This territory was left vacant by another representative that the company asked to resign, so I really didn't know what to expect. George, being a trustworthy fellow, trusted and believed in the person he hired for that territory. Unfortunately, the previous representative left the territory a mess, had alienated our once loyal customers, and had overstocked his accounts. Needless to say, George was angry with what we discovered. Since he worked with us for two to three days consecutively, I drove him back to his hotel for the night and would pick him up at 6 a.m. the next day for our third and last day together. As was George's custom, he was pacing the parking lot of the hotel smoking a cigarette when I arrived 15 minutes early to pick him up. He was his usually perky self, and we set out to our first account eager to see a surgeon at the hospital before he started surgery. After we finished with the first account, George said, "I'm buying let's go get something to eat." Having an extraordinary metabolism, George liked a hearty breakfast and his favorite place was The International House of Pancakes. He ordered a tall stack of flapjacks and started talking. He admitted that he was at fault, that he had believed and trusted Bernie too much and took the blame for the deplorable condition of the territory. Now most managers would find a person on which to place the blame, but George was a leader and shouldered the blame himself. I soon discovered that George would freely give credit to others and routinely take the blame for things needing improvement. From that point on, George never brought up the previous rep's name again, we only focused on our yearly objectives and how we could improve our sales. George accomplished that by working with me; he helped me improve, and worked closely to help win back our customers' trust. Sure enough, with George's expert leadership, within a few months the territory was back in decent shape. Each year the company did minor realignment of territories. George called me over in private at a regional meeting to tell me that he promised me when he rehired me that my territory was worth a certain dollar amount of yearly business. Since the territory was in poorer shape than he anticipated, he said he pulled strings so that the minor realignment of the territories were completed in my favor so the yearly sales would be close to what they should have been. Because George was a man of character and honor, he wanted me to have the territory he promised when he rehired me, and he did.

Great Leaders:
1. Keep promises
2. Admit mistakes
3. Make amends
4. Focus on the future

Chapter 10 – Wrong Jungle

"Be faithful in small things because it is in them that your strength lies".............Mother Teresa

Pastor Don Peterman was a prematurely graying man of God, probably in his mid fifties, and led our church congregation of about 500 parishioners. I cannot think of a more difficult task in leadership than being the patriarch of a church family where nearly everyone has a need, spiritual or otherwise. He was a man of principle who set an example of character rivaled by few others in our opinion. Pastor Peterman was always there for every need that his flock might have. Whether it was officiating at our wedding, being present during the birth of one of our children, or at the hospital when one of us had surgery, he was always there for support, moral and spiritual. In addition to his duties as senior pastor, he was a master of pastoral care. We felt that he was always available for us when a need arose, and he didn't disappoint us. He built a cadre of loyal followers, and enjoyed the support of scores of churchgoers. However there was a growing degree of dissent among six to eight members who were intent on overthrowing his church leadership. It is almost like a group attempting a coup over the leadership of a small country, there are no real winners. This became an untenable situation and as one can imagine, created enormous stress on our pastor. Within a few months he suffered a major heart attack, and eventually underwent heart bypass surgery. This proved to be a major wake-up call for Pastor Don as he embarked on his future. I was working in the surgical business at the time and would bump into him regularly at the hospital during his outpatient rehabilitation sessions. He always happily commented that he was progressing nicely and intent on adopting a new lifestyle so that he could remain healthy. I admired his tenacity especially since I fondly remembered how he and I would have breakfast occasionally at Coco's Restaurant where he would routinely order two eggs and bacon burned to a crisp. Postoperatively though, he was changing his life. This major heart attack and bypass surgery caused Pastor Don to reassess his priorities. Stephen Covey stated; "A leader is the one who climbs the tallest tree, surveys the entire situation, and yells, "Wrong jungle",[16] so Pastor Don made changes. Soon thereafter, he accepted another position a few states away, where he could concentrate on his gift of pastoral care and stepped down as senior pastor. As a family we were devastated to be losing our pastor, a man of such honor and character who meant so much to us and our children. I reminded myself of a conversation he had with me years before when he told me how much he enjoyed doing pastoral care, and ministering to a needy flock. I realized then that he was setting an example for us whereby he was shifting his priorities based on his personal need at this time in his life. He realized where he would be more effective, for both others and himself. Famous college basketball coach John Wooden said, "Do not let what you cannot do interfere with what you can do". Pastor Don came to the realization that he would be more effective in a new role that was more suited to what he could do now. He continued his ministry in that capacity for well over 20 years in another state.

I have contacted him every few years since and have always ended the conversation feeling uplifted and thankful he had such an impact on our family life. I contacted him again just a couple of years ago to see if he was doing well, since he must now be in his eighties and was greeted warmly with his trademark comment "My word", indicating his surprise that I was on the other end of the line.

We had a warm conversation, recapping what has occurred in each of our lives since our last conversation six years before. I recently was extremely saddened to hear that he passed away and went home to heaven. His obituary aptly put his life in perspective:

"Don's type A personality meant that he gave his all to whatever he was doing. His special gift was to minister to the sick and infirm—he regularly made hundreds of visits per month to those who were hospitalized or ill. Six days a week Don would call on the sick in area hospitals without fail. His great personal charisma, warmth and love for God and people endeared him to all. One special example of Don's unconditional love was the tender attention he gave to a young man dying with AIDS. When others were afraid to come close to this critically ill young man, Don faithfully visited him. Before the young man died, Don led him to believe in the Lord Jesus Christ as his personal savior. Out of gratitude for the faithful love shown to her son, the son's mother unexpectedly gifted to Don a Lincoln Town Car, a car that Don always dreamed of owning, but knew he would never be able to afford. The wheels on that car spun as Don's last ten years of life were spent visiting the sick and housebound."

> Great Leaders:
> 1. Reassess their priorities.
> 2. Tend to the needs of others.
> 3. Attract followers through trust.

Chapter 11 - Customization

"Effective leadership is not about making speeches or being liked; leadership is defined by results not attributes". ....Peter Drucker

My teaching career began with a five year stint at my old high school where my formative years developed. Our principal, Gary Perkins, was a visionary leader, as well as a competent manager. During those five years I had several conversations with Gary that proved to be very educational for me in the areas of leadership; I learned his philosophy, his methods, and his execution of principles that made him a leader to emulate.

Gary believed his primary focus should be one of a visionary. He explained many times that having a vision of where he wants to lead was a key in staying focused on his job. The visionary can see, in minds eye, where the organization will be in the future. Managers have a tougher time with this. The administrator's job is to keep focused on the desired goal, and then lead subordinates in that direction. As time passes, the leader then will continually assess the progress, make changes and tweak the system along the way. Eventually the objective will be met, or substantially met to the satisfaction of the leader. He described the process as analogous to that of a chess game. A chess master anticipates as many moves ahead as he can, then makes the highest percentage move he feels appropriate in that direction.

Gary also believes that there is a need for managerial skills to supplement one's leadership capabilities. Upon his arrival at this school in 1995, he found that the school was in financial disarray. One of his primary objectives dictated by the district was to get the fiscal house in order. In this area he utilized his leadership skills to manage the financial morass that he encountered. He stressed the importance of assessing the situation accurately so that he knew exactly what the problem was. He then mapped out a plan to balance the disparities and achieve the financial status required to effectively lead the school forward. He reiterated that there is a delicate balance between leadership and management, stating that too much of one and too little of another would not provide the most effective results. He estimated that he employed approximately 70%

leadership and 30% management in order to effectively do his job as a school administrator.

Working with Gary proved that he was somewhat task oriented. So it was not a surprise when he mentioned that astute organizational skills were required for effective leadership. He is interested in how things work, but doesn't get bogged down with micromanagement of details. He successfully delegates the task duties to capable subordinates, and manages their progress. He states that effective leaders keep their eyes on their visionary goal ahead of them and lead subordinates in that direction in an organized fashion until the goal is achieved. His method is to assess the problem, and the skill sets of the personnel under him, then alter his leadership style to get the most productive results from his subordinates. I believe he uses the situational approach to accomplish his objectives. By this I mean, he diagnoses the competency of the individuals working for him, and gauges their ability. He then adjusts his leadership style to complement the subordinate's developmental level by leading them to improve their deficiencies that will ultimately improve the production of their work. Increased production will then lead to goal achievement; that was his initial vision. He reaches two goals using this method: first he achieves the goal established in his vision; and secondly he assists people in their personal growth. He systematically identifies their level of development, then adjusts his style within the situational approach model. There have been times where he has had to employ all four styles, delegating, supporting, coaching, and directing. [17] Being a former coach, band director, and now administrator, he has found that these styles now come naturally.

Gary also proved to be thoughtful and deliberate in his leadership style. Coupled with the situational approach model, he adapts his leadership style to the developmental level of the individual. Gary explained that he preferred to implement strategies of referent leadership. He likes to get to know an individual personally, get interested in what is going on in their lives, and build a relationship. [19] As Archimedes said "Give me the ability to influence through referent power and their strong abilities will move this organization toward success." [20] He feels that he can help people grow and capitalize on this relationship and their abilities to achieve his leadership goals. He was able to comprehend what his followers want, and then creates value in their aspirations that leads to a greater sense of purpose and then he sets out to help us achieve our goals.[21] On each occasion that we talked, the first thing he always asked was "What is going on with you now Jim?" He listened intently to my response, then based on my answers, offered to help me in any way that he could. That was always the case while I worked for him; he built social power, he got people to follow him for the relationship he has established with them. He plays the win-win game, achieves his goals, helps you grow and achieve yours as well. He was a good leader to emulate.

From a personal standpoint, Gary was empathetic and caring. I went to him one Thursday morning, a little over thirteen years ago. My 84 year old father was dying, and only had days to live. I had a field trip scheduled for some students on Saturday and needed a replacement, and asked for his advice. He said "Jim, you do whatever you have to do, take all of the time that you need." He found a replacement for me, and even offered a stipend to another teacher in order to take the responsibility of my students. Dave, my replacement, was more than happy to help me out even without a stipend. I followed up with Gary to inform him that the kids would be taken care of on the trip, and Gary again assured me that I was free to spend the time I needed to tend to family business. Sure enough, Dad passed on the next afternoon. I completed the family business associated with the death of a loved one, and returned to school five or six days later. I arrived at school on the following Wednesday morning and went to retrieve my mail from my box and found on the top of the mail stack, as if it had be strategically placed there, a card on school stationary with a hand written note from Gary. His sentiments were heartfelt and touching, and he concluded by stating that although he did not personally know my dad, he must have been a great man because he knew me. This concern for the personal wellbeing of my family and I was greatly appreciated.

Great Leaders:
1. Are empathetic and caring.
2. Expressions are heartfelt.
3. Are concerned with a person's wellbeing.
4. Connect with people
5. Build relationships
6. Help people grow
7. Build social power

Chapter 12 – Getting Personal

"A mind that is stretched by a new experience can never go back to its old dimensions"..................................*Oliver Wendell Holmes, Jr.*

A few years later I returned to my local university to pursue a Master's Degree in educational leadership, I was fortunate to have several excellent instructors. One of the distinct advantages of enrolling in this particular university's program was their choice of professors. These teaching professionals have a breadth of experience in the field of education, with many of them being adjunct professors as they are still working in the field. This gave us as students a real world perspective of the field of education. One of the more engaging, salt of the earth teachers was Mr. Jeff Seymour. Mr. Seymour was a school district superintendent, and the two decades of seasoning in this position gave him a wealth of experiences to share with us. He made it a habit to know each of us and solicit our viewpoints, and carefully considered what each of us had to say. We felt as if we had ownership in the discussions, and felt free to voice our opinions. This expression of empowerment that he freely endorsed, allowed us to work in class without limits on ourselves. Mr. Seymour cultivated the conditions that created the empowering environment, which led to leveraging the unique traits that each of us possesses.[22] This is because Seymour was so secure with himself that he enjoyed discussions and felt that he could learn from all of us with whom he engaged. He wants to explore other's views, so that he can help them achieve their goals so that they both can be successful. This is best demonstrated by the method he used to replace a principal in his district who retired. Evidently this principal enjoyed her position so much in this district, and was so committed to children, that she continued on the job well into her 75th year. Suddenly Mr. Seymour needed to find a suitable replacement. He was so devoted to maintaining the culture and continuity of the school, that he said that he spent most of a week at the school asking everyone what kind of principal they wanted him to hire. I about fell off my chair that evening during class when he said he wanted to solicit everyone's opinion on who they wanted to work for. Never have I ever been asked what I wanted in a superior either in business nor education. This mindful expression of confidence in his teachers is bound to foster greater morale, dedication, and hopefully student achievement. The wisdom of Mr. Seymour granting ownership to the school personnel will most certainly increase the overall effectiveness of the school.

As with George, my manager in the medical business some 20 years earlier, Seymour freely heaped praise on those that he felt deserved it. After he graded the final exam he called me personally and left a voicemail to praise me on my performance in class and encouraged me to continue in this field. He followed it up with an email of the same theme. This praise was genuine, and specific. In acknowledging appreciation of my work, he solidified my desire to continue my diligent work efforts. By pointing out my writing performance in class, he clearly demonstrated how he truly paid close attention to my work[23]. This type of leadership yields reciprocity. A few years ago, the university's department of education presented Mr. Seymour with an award for his stellar contributions to the Educational Leadership Program, and special mention was made about him being everyone's favorite teacher. As the saying goes, "what goes around comes around" has never been more true. It is a tremendous morale booster for one to receive a personal note or call from someone they trust, complimenting them on their performance. For many years now I have sent letters to parents of students whom I have taught during the year who have exhibited the highest level of personal character and integrity in my class that year. I have always been touched and appreciative when someone compliments us on one of our children for their behavior when we are not present. I figured that these parents would appreciate it also. Each year this represents approximately 30% of my student load. I explain that their child has exhibited the highest degree of character and integrity in my class, and that is a credit to them as parents. I have received letters and tearful phone calls sometimes many weeks or months later from these parents and students telling me what this had meant and that this has never happened to them before. This leadership trait I learned from George 25 years ago and also modeled by Mr. Seymour at the university pays dividends, earns trust, and builds lifelong acquaintances.

Great Leaders:
1. Praise their workers.
2. Are secure with themselves.
3. Model behavior they desire in their workers.

Chapter 13 – Where Everybody Knows Your Name

"Management is about arranging and telling while leadership is about nurturing and inspiring."............Tom Peters

Most recently at my local university I have been greatly influenced by Dr. Phyllis Hensley. She has been invaluable as a professor and an advisor to her students. She is readily available to her students, in person, via email, and even by telephone. It started for me when I enrolled in a graduate education class taught by her in the fall of 2007. She started the course much like most teachers, reviewing the course outline and expectations, but she was different. She made it an exercise to know everyone of us personally by the end of the first session. And that she did. She bid us all farewell at the end of the evening by name, and said she looked forward to seeing us again the following week.

After several weeks the first paper was due. Students apprehensively turned in their work on that Monday evening, most with anticipation wondering if we lived up to Dr. Hensley's graduate level standards. Many of us left hoping that we wouldn't let her down. This was because, although we were with her for only three or four class sessions, she developed a level of trust with each student that made us want to do our best for her. One week later in class she returned our work, each in a personalized envelope, graded for errors, with a thoughtful, full page commentary on our work. She then allowed each student to gain full credit on the report by correcting the errors and turning in a new flawless assignment during class the following week. This technique used by Dr. Hensley showed us that she values each student's work, and by allowing us to correct mistakes we learned how to properly present a report.

For a few of us, Hensley found our work worthy enough to put together into a larger piece for possible publication. She invited five of us to work a little overtime to develop an article. We met weekly with her for several weeks to fine tune our article, with the hopes of publication in the future. Due to an unexpected medical leave, Dr. Hensley was not able to continue the process. Yet, when she resumed working in the fall of 2008 she contacted us right away to continue the advancement of getting our article published. She even bestowed us with the honor of presenting our article before an organization where she served as president. Dr. Hensley establishes a personal relationship with all students, fostering unique talents in each of us that inspire achievement beyond our own expectations. Although demanding and a perfectionist, Dr. Hensley astutely leads all students to higher levels of accomplishment. She often says "I see you doing this or that, but you just don't know it yet." This is emblematic of a great mentor and leader. Dr. Hensley empowers us through a trusting and caring relationship. Her capacity to trust others earns her greater trust in return. [24] She guides us in a direction she knows we can be skillful in, and cultivates the fertile ground for us. By nurturing our growth, she leads us to excel at levels that we couldn't achieve on our own.

> Great Leaders:
>   1. Cultivate ground for their workers.
>   2. Nurture workers as they grow.
>   3. Identifies strengths, and guides workers in that direction.

Epilogue

Although each of these scenarios is uniquely different in their own way, they are alike at the same time as well. The core of each of these leaders is strikingly similar in many respects. Each leader established a personal trusting relationship with me and in most cases with my family, each had robust relationships in their personal lives, and even occasionally introduced me and my family to their other acquaintances. All lead with their heart and trust their judgment in their relationships. They understand that it is the person of higher authority who is responsible for establishing the trusting relationship.

Each of these role models has always exhibited the highest degree of integrity and character in their dealings with not only me, but others as well. Each recognized my gifts and unique traits and nurtured me as I strove to improve my craft. They understand what American urban studies theorist, Richard Florida believes, namely that" people don't need to be managed, they need to be unleashed."

These leaders often exploited my talents that I did not know I had for my benefit, and were encouraging and helpful in the process. They understand that by helping their subordinates become more successful, they too will realize greater success and growth as well.

Finally each of these role models has solid family relationships, some already built from prior generations, and most have planted the same seeds for generations to come. They have simply transferred this trait to people in their professional lives of whom they lead. It reminds me of a story I read years ago in Readers Digest where a man was struggling in his life and sought help from a trusted uncle. This uncle gave his nephew a puzzle of a man to put together. It was one of those 1000 piece puzzles that took hours to complete. Once finished, he returned it to his uncle. What the nephew did not know was that there was a picture of a globe on the reverse side. The uncle examined the man on the completed puzzle and told his nephew to turn it over. He said, "See, when you put the man together his world falls into place." Each of these leader/role models has their lives together, and their worlds have fallen into place. They have simply passed their wisdom onto us.

About the Author

Jim is an educator, author, and biologist in Southern California. He graduated from California State Polytechnic University in Pomona, California with a Bachelor of Science degree in biology and a Master of Arts degree in Educational Leadership. For 50 years he has worked in various fields for scores of managers and a few real leaders. It is these leaders who have helped shape his outlook and career.

Book Review

Thank you again for reading this book. If you have found it helpful and enjoyed reading it, I would greatly appreciate it if you would leave a favorable review on Amazon.com so that others can be inspired by your reaction too. Also I would like to hear from you should you have inspirational stories that you would be willing to pass along. You can reach me at jim@biologistjim.com. Thanks again

References

[1] Hensley, P. A., & Burmeister, L. (2009). *Leadership connectors: Six keys to developing relationships in schools*. Larchmont, NY: Eye on Education.

[2] Sutton, R. I. (2007). *The no asshole rule: Building a civilized workplace and surviving one that isn't*. New York: Warner Business Books.

[3] Crew, R. (2007). *Only connect: The way to save our schools*. New York: Sarah Crichton Books/Farrar, Straus and Giroux.

[4,5,6,15] Miller, H. J., Garciduenas, R., Green, R., Shatola, K., & Inumba, E. (2008). What teachers want in their leaders: Voices from the field. *Educational Leadership and Administration, 20*, 57-63

[4] Hoy, W. K., & Miskel, C. G. (2008). *Educational administration: Theory, research, and practice* (8th ed.). New York: McGraw-Hill.

[7] Nelson, B. (1995). Rewarding people and performance. *R & D Innovator, 4*(1), 1-3.

[8] Sassaman, R., Cicerone, B., & Swinney, J. (2007, December 3). Reward employees for their good work - Business management - Extra edition -. *Air Conditioning, Heating & Refrigeration NEWS*. Retrieved August 31, 2009, from http://www.achrnews.com/Articles/Business_Management/B NP_GUID_9-5-2006_A_10000000000000211763

[9, 10] Maxwell, J. C. (2007). *The 21 Irrefutable laws of leadership: Follow them and people will follow you*. Nashville: Thomas Nelson.

[11] Peters, T. J. (1984). *In search of excellence lessons from America's best-run companies*. New York, NY: Warner Books.

[12] Covey, S. M., & Merrill, R. R. (2006). *The speed of trust: The one thing that changes everything*. New York: Free Press.

[13] Iacocca, L. (2007). *Where have all the leaders gone?* New York: Scribner.

[14] Cox, D., & Hoover, J. (1992). *Leadership when the heat's on*. New York: McGraw-Hill.

[16] Covey, S. R. (1989). *The 7 habits of highly effective people*. New York: Fireside.

[17, 18] Northouse, P. G. (2006). *Leadership theory and practice* (4th ed.). Minneapolis: Sage Publications, Inc.

[19] Thomas, J. C. (2002). Leadership effectiveness of referent power as a distinction of personal power. *Regent University Center of Leadership Studies*, 1-11.

[20] Mannering, D. E., & Wilde, K. D. (1989). *How good managers become great leaders*. Danbury: Options Unlimited, Incorporated.

[21] Burns, J. M. (2003). *Transforming leadership: The pursuit of happiness*. New York: Atlantic Monthly Press.

[22] Covey, S. R., Merrill, A. R., & Merrill, R. R. (1994). *First things first: To live, to love, to learn, to leave a legacy*. New York: Simon & Schuster.

[23] Britto, C. (n.d.). Employee Praise | Praising Employees | 5 Ways To Give Praise | Leadership In Action. *Coaching - Leadership executive coaching - Executive coach - Performance coaching - CMOE*. Retrieved August 30, 2009,

from http://www.cmoe.com/blog/5-ways-to-give-praise-

small-efforts-with-a-huge-return.htm .

[24] Reina, D. S. (2006). *Trust and betrayal in the workplace building*

effective relationships in your organizations. San Francisco,

CA: Berrett-Koehler.